GIANT
COCKTAILS

GIANT
COCKTAILS

PARTY DRINKS, PUNCH BOWLS, AND OTHER BEVERAGES TO SHARE

25 DELICIOUS RECIPES PERFECT FOR GROUPS

ÉMILIE LARAISON

Skyhorse Publishing

Author's Note

I love parties and inviting a lot of people over: family, friends, friends of friends . . . basically, I love a party with good people.

I also like everything to be ready in advance so I can have fun with my guests and enjoy my time with them.

If you're like me, why not make several giant cocktails beforehand so everyone can help themselves to refreshing drinks all night long? This book has recipes with and without alcohol to make all of your guests happy.

All you need are a few tools, some glasses, fruit, juices, sodas, spices, and your favorite alcohols, and you're ready to go!

Are you ready to mix it up? In this book I'm going to show you my personal twist on a few of the classics, some chic cocktails, tropical drinks, and other cocktails that the dessert lovers among your friends will love. No matter what kind of party you're having, you'll find just the the right drink!

Serve your guests a delicious cocktail as soon as they arrive—it's a great way to start the party!

Show off your mixology skills and prepare delicious strawberry daiquiris, elegant bubbly champagne punch, or maybe a refreshing raspberry-rosé sangria. Get them ready just before your guests arrive (make sure you have plenty of ice cubes on hand to keep them cold) and set them out in large bowls so everyone can serve themselves!

Giant cocktails and good times with old and new friends . . . Sounds great to me!

Émilie Laraison

Who am I?
I have been an author and food stylist for ten years. I love food that is healthy, simple, and flavorful. I enjoy inventing recipes that are wholesome, delicious, and creative as a way to share my passion for modern gastronomy.

Contents

Kitten Kiss

MAKES 10 TALL DRINKS

Preparation: 15–20 minutes

Refrigeration: 2 hours

EQUIPMENT

Cocktail spoon

Mixer

Conical strainer

Funnel

1 empty 34 fl oz (1 l) bottle

Ingredients
For 34 fl oz (1 l) of shrub
(tangy fruit syrup):

2½ oz (70 g) red pepper

3½ oz (100 g) raspberries, fresh or frozen

5 fl oz (15 cl) balsamic vinegar

7 oz (200 g) sugar

8 fl oz water

For the cocktail:

13½ fl oz (40 cl) vodka

6¾ fl oz (20 cl) lemon juice

10 fl oz (30 cl) balsamic raspberry-pepper shrub

Around 60 ice cubes

34 fl oz (1 l) ginger ale

Prepare the shrub. Wash and deseed the red peppers. Put all of the ingredients in the bowl of a mixer with 8½ fl oz (25 cl) of water. Mix on high for 1 minute. Strain the mixture and pour into the empty bottle with the help of the funnel (the shrub will keep in the refrigerator for 1 month).

Now prepare the cocktail. Combine the vodka, lemon juice, and 10 fl oz (30 cl) of the shrub in a large bowl. Place 4 or 5 ice cubes in each glass then pour the mixture over them.

Stir with a cocktail spoon for 10 to 15 seconds to cool the ingredients. Add the ginger ale directly to each glass.

Serve chilled.

LES Justes
PIGALLE

1 rue Frochot, Paris 75009

Les Justes is a "neighborhood" cocktail bar with ethical and responsible practices that is close to its customers' hearts. Being *"juste,"* or "fair," is more than just a concept and is the mantra of this cozy and welcoming establishment.

FIRST THINGS
FIRST . . .

Tools You Need To Make Cocktails At Home!

1 Citrus reamer for juicing

2 Grater for zesting citrus

3 Muddler to maximize flavor

4 Knife for cutting fruit

5 Cocktail spoon for mixing

6 Corkscrew for opening bottles

7 Large bowls for serving cocktails

8 Glasses of different sizes for serving

9 Conical Strainer

+ Blender/mixer for crushing ice and mixing ingredients

Basic Tips

Juices are always better when you make them yourself, but you can certainly still use bottled juice. Just make sure to buy ones that are "100% juice."

Decorate and garnish your glasses with things that go with your cocktail, like pieces of fruit, fresh herbs, or a dash of spice, or frost the rim of the glass by dipping it in liqueur or syrup followed by sugar or salt and repeating this process several times, depending on your recipe.

Ice is a very important part of any cocktail and should be as cold as possible so it doesn't water down the mixture.

Refrigerate your drinks and fruit 2 hours before preparing the cocktail so it will be at the right temperature for serving.

Set up a bar with the basic liquors so you can make all kinds of giant cocktails.

Make something to snack on: a few dips, spreads, and some toasted slices of bread!

Plan for a variety of different cocktails and snacks so all your guests will find something they like.

A Basic Step-by-Step Recipe: Mojito

SERVES 10
Preparation: 10 minutes
EQUIPMENT
Muddler
Blender
Knife

INGREDIENTS
6 cold limes

1 bunch mint

3½ oz (100 g) brown sugar

13½ fl oz (40 cl) lime juice, chilled

25 fl oz (70 cl) white rum

8½ fl oz (25 cl) sparkling water, chilled

Around 20 ice cubes

Cut the limes into pieces and wash the mint leaves.

Place the mint leaves (set aside a few for decoration), brown sugar, and lime juice in a large bowl and crush with a muddler.

Crush the ice using a blender or rolling pin.

Add the lime pieces, rum, and crushed ice to the bowl.

Finish with sparkling water and decorate with mint leaves.

Alcohol-free
For a virgin mojito, just replace the rum with lemonade.

THE CLASSICS

Cuba Libre

MAKES 10 GLASSES

Preparation: 5 minutes

EQUIPMENT

Cocktail spoon

Citrus reamer

Knife

INGREDIENTS

10 cold limes

20 fl oz (60 cl) dark rum

Around 20 ice cubes

40½ fl oz (1.2 l) cola, chilled

5 mint sprigs

2 inches (5 cm) fresh ginger

Juice 5 limes. Pour the rum and lime juice into a large bowl. Add the ice cubes. Stir using a cocktail spoon then add the cola.

Wash and dry the mint leaves. Peel the ginger and slice into thin rounds. Add these to the bowl. Rinse the remaining limes and cut them in quarters. Add them to the cocktail.

Serve chilled.

Alcohol-Free Version

INGREDIENTS

10 cold limes

2 vanilla beans

Around 20 ice cubes

40½ fl oz (1.2 l) cola, chilled

17 fl oz (50 cl) lemonade, chilled

3⅓ fl oz (10 cl) sugarcane syrup

5 mint sprigs

2 inches (5 cm) fresh ginger

Juice 5 limes. Slice the vanilla beans in half lengthwise. Scrape out the seeds using the tip of a knife.

Put the ice cubes in a large bowl. Pour in the cola, lemonade, lime juice, and sugarcane syrup. Then add the vanilla bean seeds. Stir with a cocktail spoon.

Wash and dry the mint leaves. Peel the ginger and slice into thin rounds. Add these to the bowl. Rinse the remaining limes and cut them in quarters. Add them to the cocktail.

Serve chilled.

Fresh Peach Gin and Tonic

MAKES 10 GLASSES

Preparation: 5 minutes

EQUIPMENT

Muddler

Cocktail spoon

Knife

INGREDIENTS

5 cold lemons

Around 20 ice cubes

13½ fl oz (40 cl) gin

27 fl oz (80 cl) tonic water, chilled

3⅓ fl oz (10 cl) peach syrup

5 cold peaches

5 thyme sprigs

Rinse the lemons and slice them in rounds. Add to a large bowl with the ice cubes. Gently muddle then pour in the gin, tonic, and peach syrup. Stir with a cocktail spoon.

Wash the peaches and cut them in quarters. Wash and dry the thyme sprigs. Add the peaches and thyme to the cocktail.

Serve chilled.

Alcohol-Free Version

INGREDIENTS

5 cold lemons

Around 20 ice cubes

40½ fl oz (1.2 l) tonic water, chilled

3⅓ fl oz (10 cl) peach syrup

5 cold peaches

5 thyme sprigs

Rinse the lemons and slice them in rounds. Add to a large bowl with the ice cubes. Gently muddle then pour in the tonic and syrup. Stir with a cocktail spoon.

Wash the peaches and cut them in quarters. Wash and dry the thyme sprigs. Add the peaches and thyme to the cocktail.

Serve chilled.

Caipirinha

MAKES 10 GLASSES
Preparation: 5 minutes

EQUIPMENT

Muddler

Blender

Cocktail spoon

INGREDIENTS

Around 100 ice cubes

10 cold limes

14 oz (400 g) cane sugar

25 fl oz (75 cl) cachaça

5 mint sprigs

Blend the ice cubes to make crushed ice.

Rinse the limes and cut each one into 8 pieces. Add to a large bowl and cover with sugar. Muddle to extract the lime juice. Add the crushed ice, then the cachaça. Mix with a cocktail spoon.

Wash and dry the mint leaves. Add to the cocktail.

Serve chilled.

Alcohol-Free Version

INGREDIENTS

Around 100 ice cubes

10 cold limes

10½ oz (300 g) cane sugar

28¾ fl oz (85 cl) tonic water, chilled

5 mint sprigs

Blend the ice cubes to make crushed ice.

Rinse the limes and cut each one into 8 pieces. Add to a large bowl and cover with sugar. Muddle to extract the lime juice. Add the crushed ice and tonic water. Mix with a cocktail spoon.

Wash and dry the mint leaves. Add to the cocktail.

Serve chilled.

Strawberry Daiquiri

—

MAKES 10 GLASSES

Preparation: 10 minutes

EQUIPMENT

Blender

Knife

INGREDIENTS

18 oz (500 g) cold strawberries

17 fl oz (50 cl) white rum

10 fl oz (30 cl) lime juice, chilled

1¾ fl oz (5 cl) sugarcane syrup

6¾ fl oz (20 cl) strawberry liqueur

Around 20 ice cubes

3 cold limes

5 basil sprigs

Wash the strawberries and remove the stems. Set a few aside for decoration and put the rest in a blender with the rum, lime juice, syrup, and liqueur. Blend. Add the ice cubes and blend again. Pour into a large bowl.

Cut the decorative strawberries in half and slice the limes. Wash and dry the basil. Slice limes into rounds and decorate the cocktail with the rounds, strawberries, and basil leaves.

Serve chilled.

Alcohol-Free Version

INGREDIENTS

26½ oz (750 g) cold strawberries

10 fl oz (30 cl) lime juice, chilled

3⅓ fl oz (10 cl) strawberry syrup

1¾ fl oz (5 cl) sugarcane syrup

Around 20 ice cubes

10 fl oz (30 cl) sparkling water, chilled

5 basil sprigs

3 cold limes

Remove the strawberry stems. Set aside a few berries for decoration and place the rest in a blender with the lime juice and syrups. Blend. Add the ice cubes and blend again. Pour in the sparkling water. Transfer the mixture to a large bowl.

Cut the decorative strawberries in half and slice the limes. Wash and dry the basil. Decorate with lime rounds, strawberries, and basil leaves.

Serve chilled.

Raspberry-Rosé Sangria

MAKES 20 GLASSES

Preparation: 5 minutes

EQUIPMENT

Blender

Cocktail spoon

INGREDIENTS

Around 20 ice cubes

2 bottles rosé, chilled

2⅓ fl oz (7 cl) crème de framboise or raspberry liqueur

40½ fl oz (1.2 l) sparkling water, chilled

5 mint sprigs

9 oz (250 g) cold raspberries

Blend the ice to make crushed ice.

Put the ice in a large bowl. Pour in the rosé and the crème de framboise. Add the sparkling water. Stir with a cocktail spoon.

Wash and dry the mint leaves. Add the raspberries and mint to the bowl.

Serve chilled.

Alcohol-Free Version

INGREDIENTS

Around 20 ice cubes

34 fl oz (1 l) red grape juice, chilled

20 fl oz (60 cl) raspberry juice, chilled

40½ fl oz (1.2 l) sparkling water, chilled

5 mint sprigs

9 oz (250 g) cold raspberries

Blend the ice to make crushed ice.

Put the ice in a large bowl. Pour in the grape and raspberry juice. Add the sparkling water. Stir with a cocktail spoon.

Wash and dry the mint leaves. Add the raspberries and mint to the bowl.

Serve chilled.

Bloody Mary

EQUIPMENT

Cocktail spoon

Knife

INGREDIENTS

Around 20 ice cubes

3⅓ fl oz (10 cl) lemon juice, chilled

1 tsp cayenne pepper

1¾ fl oz (5 cl) Tabasco® sauce

1¾ fl oz (5 cl) Worcestershire sauce

1 cold head of celery

1 tsp celery salt

Pepper, to taste

17 fl oz (50 cl) vodka

34 fl oz (1 l) tomato juice, chilled

Place the ice cubes in a large bowl. Add the lemon juice. Add the cayenne pepper, sauces, salt, and pepper. Next pour in the vodka and tomato juice. Stir with a cocktail spoon.

Wash and chop the celery stalks and place them on the side of the bowl for your guests to stir their drinks.

Serve chilled.

Alcohol-Free Version

INGREDIENTS

Around 20 ice cubes

3⅓ fl oz (10 cl) lemon juice, chilled

1 tsp cayenne pepper

1¾ fl oz (5 cl) Tabasco® sauce

1¾ fl oz (5 cl) Worcestershire sauce

1 tsp celery salt

Pepper, to taste

51 fl oz (1.5 l) tomato juice, chilled

1 cold head of celery

Place the ice cubes in a large bowl. Add the lemon juice. Add the cayenne pepper, sauces, salt, and pepper. Next pour in the tomato juice. Stir with a cocktail spoon.

Wash and chop the celery stalks and place them on the side of the bowl for your guests to stir their drinks.

Serve chilled.

Grapefruit Long Island Iced Tea

MAKES 10 GLASSES

Preparation: 5 minutes

EQUIPMENT

Cocktail spoon

Knife

INGREDIENTS

Around 20 ice cubes

5 fl oz (15 cl) vodka

5 fl oz (15 cl) gin

5 fl oz (15 cl) Cointreau®

5 fl oz (15 cl) tequila

3⅓ fl oz (10 cl) grapefruit syrup

10 fl oz (30 cl) grapefruit juice, chilled

17 fl oz (50 cl) cola (or iced tea), chilled

1 cold grapefruit

Place the ice cubes in a large bowl.

Add the vodka, gin, Cointreau®, and tequila and stir with a cocktail spoon. Add the grapefruit syrup and juice. Finish with the cola. Mix.

Wash and slice the grapefruit. Add the slices to the bowl.

Serve chilled.

Alcohol-Free Version

INGREDIENTS

Around 20 ice cubes

10 fl oz (30 cl) iced tea

10 fl oz (30 cl) grapefruit juice, chilled

3⅓ fl oz (10 cl) grapefruit syrup

17 fl oz (50 cl) cola (or iced tea), chilled

10 fl oz (30 cl) lemonade, chilled

1 cold grapefruit

Place the ice cubes in a large bowl.

Add the iced tea, grapefruit syrup, and juice. Stir with a cocktail spoon. Finish with the cola and lemonade. Mix.

Wash and slice the grapefruit. Add the slices to the bowl.

Serve chilled.

Americano

EQUIPMENT

Cocktail spoon

Knife

INGREDIENTS

1 cold orange

2 cold lemons

Around 20 ice cubes

13½ fl oz (40 cl) Campari®

13½ fl oz (40 cl) red vermouth

20 fl oz (60 cl) sparkling water, chilled

Rinse and slice the lemons and orange. Add to a large bowl with the ice cubes.

Add the Campari® and vermouth, then add the sparkling water. Stir with a cocktail spoon.

Serve chilled.

Alcohol-Free Version

INGREDIENTS

1 cold orange

2 cold lemons

Around 20 ice cubes

6¾ fl oz (20 cl) grenadine syrup

17 fl oz (50 cl) orange juice, chilled

25 fl oz (70 cl) sparkling water, chilled

Rinse and slice the lemons and orange. Add to a large bowl with the ice cubes.

Add the grenadine syrup and orange juice then pour in the sparkling water. Stir with a cocktail spoon.

Serve chilled.

Bellini

MAKES 10 GLASSES

Preparation: 5 minutes

EQUIPMENT

Cocktail spoon

Knife

INGREDIENTS

Around 20 ice cubes

17 fl oz (50 cl) peach purée, chilled

1¾ fl oz (5 cl) sugarcane syrup

25 fl oz (75 cl) champagne (or sparkling white wine), chilled

4 cold white peaches

Place the ice cubes in a large bowl. Pour in the peach purée and sugarcane syrup and stir with a cocktail spoon. Add the champagne and gently mix.

Wash and slice the peaches. Add to the cocktail.

Serve chilled.

Alcohol-Free Version

INGREDIENTS

Around 20 ice cubes

17 fl oz (50 cl) peach purée, chilled

1¾ fl oz (5 cl) sugarcane syrup

6¾ fl oz (20 cl) white grape juice, chilled

20 fl oz (60 cl) sparkling water, chilled

4 cold white peaches

Place the ice cubes in a large bowl. Pour in the peach purée and sugarcane syrup and stir with a cocktail spoon. Add the white grape juice and sparkling water. Gently mix.

Wash and slice the peaches. Add to the cocktail.

Serve chilled.

EVENING
ATTIRE

Aperol Spritz

MAKES 10 GLASSES

Preparation: 5 minutes

EQUIPMENT

Cocktail spoon

Knife

Toothpicks

INGREDIENTS

Around 20 ice cubes

13½ fl oz (40 cl) Aperol®

20 fl oz (60 cl) sparkling white wine (prosecco), chilled

6¾ fl oz (20 cl) sparkling water, chilled

3 cold lemons

2 cold blood oranges

10 green olives

Place the ice cubes in a large bowl. Pour in the Aperol® and stir with a cocktail spoon. Add the sparkling white wine and water. Mix.

Wash the lemons and oranges and slice in rounds. Add these to the cocktail.

Serve chilled with 1 green olive on a toothpick for each glass.

Alcohol-Free Version

INGREDIENTS

Around 20 ice cubes

13½ fl oz (40 cl) blood orange juice, chilled

6¾ fl oz (20 cl) white grape juice, chilled

3 cold lemons

2 cold blood oranges

20 fl oz (60 cl) sparkling water, chilled

10 green olives

Place the ice cubes in a large bowl. Pour in the juices and stir with a cocktail spoon. Add the sparkling water. Mix.

Wash the lemons and oranges and slice in rounds. Add these to the cocktail.

Serve chilled with 1 green olive on a toothpick for each glass.

Bubbly Champagne Punch

MAKES 10 GLASSES
Preparation: 5 minutes
EQUIPMENT
Cocktail spoon
Knife

INGREDIENTS

Around 20 ice cubes

5 fl oz (15 cl) white rum

6¾ fl oz (20 cl) lemon juice, chilled

1 tsp vanilla extract

3⅓ fl oz (10 cl) sugarcane syrup

25 fl oz (75 cl) champagne, chilled

17 fl oz (50 cl) tonic water, chilled

2 cold limes

5 cold oranges

9 oz (250 g) cold raspberries

5 mint sprigs

Place the ice cubes in a large bowl. Add the rum, lemon juice, vanilla extract, and syrup. Stir with a cocktail spoon. Add the champagne and tonic. Mix.

Wash and slice the limes and oranges. Add to the cocktail along with the raspberries. Wash and dry the mint leaves and add to the bowl.

Serve chilled.

Alcohol-Free Version

INGREDIENTS

Around 20 ice cubes

6¾ fl oz (20 cl) lemon juice, chilled

5 fl oz (15 cl) white grape juice, chilled

1 tsp vanilla extract

3⅓ fl oz (10 cl) sugarcane syrup

25 fl oz (75 cl) sparkling water, chilled

17 fl oz (50 cl) tonic water, chilled

9 oz (250 g) cold raspberries

2 cold limes

5 cold oranges

5 mint sprigs

Place the ice cubes in a large bowl. Add the lemon juice, grape juice, vanilla extract, and syrup. Stir with a cocktail spoon. Add the sparkling water and tonic. Mix.

Wash and slice the limes and oranges, add to the cocktail with the raspberries. Wash and dry the mint leaves and add to the bowl.

Serve chilled.

Cosmopolitan

MAKES 10 GLASSES

Preparation: 10 minutes

EQUIPMENT

Cocktail spoon

Grater

INGREDIENTS

Around 20 ice cubes

13½ fl oz (40 cl) vodka

13½ fl oz (40 cl) triple sec

6¾ fl oz (20 cl) lime juice, chilled

17 fl oz (50 cl) cranberry juice, chilled

1 cold orange

1¾ oz (50 g) white sugar

Place the ice cubes in a large bowl. Add the vodka and triple sec. Stir with a cocktail spoon. Add the lime and cranberry juices and stir.

Wash the orange and grate wide strips of peel. Add these to the cocktail.

Dampen the rims of the glasses and dip in sugar.

Serve chilled.

Alcohol-Free Version

Around 20 ice cubes

17 fl oz (50 cl) cranberry juice, chilled

13½ fl oz (40 cl) orange juice, chilled

6¾ fl oz (20 cl) lime juice, chilled

13½ fl oz (40 cl) tonic water, chilled

1 cold orange

1¾ oz (50 g) white sugar

Place the ice cubes in a large bowl. Pour in the juices and stir with a cocktail spoon. Add the tonic and stir.

Wash the orange and grate wide strips of peel. Add these to the cocktail.

Dampen the rims of the glasses and dip in sugar.

Serve chilled.

Moscow Mule

MAKES 10 GLASSES

Preparation: 10 minutes

EQUIPMENT

Cocktail spoon

Grater

Knife

INGREDIENTS

Around 20 ice cubes

15¼ fl oz (45 cl) vodka

1¾ fl oz (5 cl) lime juice, chilled

40½ fl oz (1.2 l) ginger beer, chilled

2 limes

½ cold cucumber

Place the ice cubes in a large bowl. Pour in the vodka and lime juice and stir with a cocktail spoon. Add the ginger beer. Mix.

Wash and zest the limes. Rinse the cucumber and slice thinly. Add the lime zest and cucumber slices to the cocktail.

Serve chilled.

Alcohol-Free Version

INGREDIENTS

Around 20 ice cubes

1¾ fl oz (5 cl) lime juice, chilled

51 fl oz (1.5 l) ginger beer, chilled

6¾ fl oz (20 cl) tonic water, chilled

2 limes

½ cold cucumber

Place the ice cubes in a large bowl. Pour in the lime juice and stir with a cocktail spoon. Add the ginger beer and tonic. Mix.

Wash and zest the limes. Rinse the cucumber and slice thinly. Add the lime zest and cucumber slices to the cocktail.

Serve chilled.

Pomegranate St. Germain

MAKES 10 GLASSES

Preparation: 10 minutes

EQUIPMENT

Cocktail spoon

Knife

INGREDIENTS

Around 20 ice cubes

*13½ fl oz (40 cl) St. Germain®
elderflower liqueur*

*10 fl oz (30 cl) pomegranate
juice, chilled*

20 fl oz (60 cl) brut prosecco, chilled

*10 fl oz (30 cl) sparkling water,
chilled*

4 cold limes

1 cold pomegranate

Place the ice cubes in a large bowl. Pour in the St. Germain®
and the pomegranate juice and stir with a cocktail spoon. Add
the prosecco and sparkling water. Gently mix.

Wash the limes and slice into rounds. Open the pomegranate
and remove the seeds. Place the lime rounds and
pomegranate seeds in the bowl.

Serve chilled.

Alcohol-Free Version

INGREDIENTS

Around 20 ice cubes

3⅓ fl oz (10 cl) elderflower syrup

*13½ fl oz (40 cl) white grape
juice, chilled*

*10 fl oz (30 cl) pomegranate
juice, chilled*

*25 fl oz (70 cl) sparkling water,
chilled*

4 cold limes

1 cold pomegranate

Place the ice cubes in a large bowl. Pour in the elderflower
syrup and fruit juices then stir with a cocktail spoon. Add the
sparkling water. Gently mix.

Wash the limes and slice into rounds. Open the pomegranate
and remove the seeds. Place the lime rounds and
pomegranate seeds in the bowl.

Serve chilled.

Mango-Blackberry Vodka

MAKES 10 GLASSES

Preparation: 5 minutes

EQUIPMENT

Blender

Knife

INGREDIENTS

Around 20 ice cubes

6¾ fl oz (20 cl) crème de mûre

17 fl oz (50 cl) mango juice, chilled

17 fl oz (50 cl) vodka

6¾ fl oz (20 cl) lemon juice, chilled

4½ oz (125 g) cold blackberries

1 cold mango

Place the ice cubes in a large bowl. Pour in the crème de mûre. Blend the mango juice with the vodka and lemon juice. Pour into the bowl without stirring. Add the blackberries to the bowl.

Wash and slice the mango to decorate the glasses.

Serve chilled.

Alcohol-Free Version

INGREDIENTS

Around 20 ice cubes

15¼ fl oz (45 cl) blackberry juice, chilled

25 fl oz (75 cl) mango juice, chilled

6¾ fl oz (20 cl) lemon juice, chilled

4½ oz (125 g) cold blackberries

1 cold mango

Place the ice cubes in a large bowl. Pour in the blackberry juice. Blend the mango juice with the lemon juice. Pour into the bowl without stirring. Add the blackberries to the bowl.

Wash and slice the mango to decorate the glasses.

Serve chilled.

TROPICAL
DREAMS

Sex on the Beach

MAKES 10 GLASSES

Preparation: 10 minutes

EQUIPMENT

Cocktail spoon

Knife

Toothpicks

INGREDIENTS

Around 20 ice cubes

13½ fl oz (40 cl) vodka

3⅓ fl oz (10 cl) raspberry liqueur

17 fl oz (50 cl) cranberry juice, chilled

3⅓ fl oz (10 cl) crème de pêche

17 fl oz (50 cl) orange juice, chilled

2 cold oranges

10 cold raspberries

Place the ice cubes in a large bowl. Pour in the vodka, raspberry liqueur, and cranberry juice. Stir with a cocktail spoon. Finish with the crème de pêche and the orange juice. Do not mix.

Wash the oranges and slice into half-rounds.

Place 1 orange half-round and 1 raspberry on each toothpick. Set aside to decorate the glasses.

Serve chilled.

Alcohol-Free Version

INGREDIENTS

Around 20 ice cubes

13½ fl oz (40 cl) raspberry juice, chilled

17 fl oz (50 cl) cranberry juice, chilled

6¾ fl oz (20 cl) peach juice, chilled

17 fl oz (50 cl) orange juice, chilled

2 cold oranges

10 cold raspberries

Place the ice cubes in a large bowl. Pour in the raspberry and cranberry juices. Stir with a cocktail spoon. Finish with the peach and orange juices. Do not mix.

Wash the oranges and slice into half-rounds.

Place 1 orange half-round and 1 raspberry on each toothpick. Set aside to decorate the glasses.

Serve chilled.

Passion Fruit Mojito

MAKES 10 GLASSES

Preparation: 10 minutes

EQUIPMENT

Blender

Muddler

Cocktail Spoon

Knife

INGREDIENTS

Around 50 ice cubes

10 mint sprigs

9 oz (250 g) cane sugar

17 fl oz (50 cl) white rum

8½ fl oz (25 cl) lime juice, chilled

8½ fl oz (25 cl) tonic water, chilled

10 cold passion fruits

Blend the ice cubes to make crushed ice.

Wash and dry the mint leaves. Place half at the bottom of a large bowl with the sugar and muddle. Add the crushed ice then pour in the rum and lime juice and mix with a cocktail spoon. Add the tonic.

Cut the passion fruits in half, remove the pulp, and add it to the bowl with the remaining mint.

Serve chilled.

Alcohol-Free Version

INGREDIENTS

Around 50 ice cubes

10 mint sprigs

9 oz (250 g) cane sugar

8½ fl oz (25 cl) pineapple juice, chilled

8½ fl oz (25 cl) lime juice, chilled

17 fl oz (50 cl) tonic water, chilled

10 cold passion fruits

Blend the ice cubes to make crushed ice.

Wash and dry the mint leaves. Place half at the bottom of a large bowl with the sugar and muddle. Add the crushed ice then pour in the lime and pineapple juices and mix with a cocktail spoon. Add the tonic.

Cut the passion fruits in half, remove the pulp, and add it to the bowl with the remaining mint.

Serve chilled.

Mai Tai

MAKES 20 GLASSES

Preparation: 5 minutes

EQUIPMENT

Cocktail spoon

Blender

Toothpicks

Knife

INGREDIENTS

Around 20 ice cubes
8½ fl oz (25 cl) Cointreau®
25 fl oz (75 cl) blood orange
juice, chilled
25 fl oz (75 cl) pineapple juice,
chilled
8½ fl oz (25 cl) white rum
8½ fl oz (25 cl) dark rum
3⅓ fl oz (10 cl) orgeat syrup
2 cold limes
2 cold oranges

Place the ice cubes in a large bowl. Pour in the Cointreau® and orange juice. Stir with a cocktail spoon.

Blend the pineapple juice with the rums and orgeat syrup. Pour into the bowl without stirring.

Slice each lime into eight pieces. Cut the oranges in wedges. Arrange on toothpicks and add to the cocktail.

Serve chilled.

Alcohol-Free Version

INGREDIENTS

Around 20 ice cubes
34 fl oz (1 l) blood orange juice,
chilled
1¾ fl oz (5 cl) orange syrup
25 fl oz (75 cl) pineapple juice,
chilled
3⅓ fl oz (10 cl) orgeat syrup
17 fl oz (50 cl) tonic water, chilled
2 cold limes
2 cold oranges

Place the ice cubes in a large bowl. Pour in the orange syrup and orange juice. Stir with a cocktail spoon.

Blend the pineapple juice with the orgeat syrup. Add the tonic and gently mix. Pour into the bowl without stirring.

Slice each lime into eight pieces. Cut the oranges in wedges. Arrange on toothpicks and add to the cocktail.

Serve chilled.

Blueberry-Cilantro Margarita

MAKES 10 GLASSES

Preparation: 5 minutes

EQUIPMENT

Cocktail spoon

Knife

INGREDIENTS

Around 20 ice cubes

27 fl oz (80 cl) tequila

13½ fl oz (40 cl) triple sec

13½ fl oz (40 cl) lime juice, chilled

10 cilantro sprigs

4½ oz (125 g) cold blueberries

5 cold limes

Salt

Place the ice cubes in a large bowl. Pour in the tequila and triple sec. Add the lime juice. Stir with a cocktail spoon.

Wash and dry the cilantro. Add to the bowl along with the blueberries. Cut the limes in rounds, then cut each round in half. Add the half-rounds to the bowl (set aside a few for decoration).

Run a slice of lime around the rim of each glass and dip in salt. Place one lime half-round on each glass for decoration.

Serve chilled.

Alcohol-Free Version

INGREDIENTS

Around 20 ice cubes

27 fl oz (80 cl) tonic water, chilled

13½ fl oz (40 cl) orange juice, chilled

13½ fl oz (40 cl) lime juice, chilled

10 cilantro sprigs

4½ oz (125 g) cold blueberries

5 cold limes

Salt

Place the ice cubes in a large bowl. Pour in the tonic and orange juice. Add the lime juice. Stir with a cocktail spoon.

Wash and dry the cilantro. Add to the bowl along with the blueberries. Cut the limes in rounds, then cut each round in half. Add the half-rounds to the bowl (set aside a few for decoration).

Run a slice of lime around the rim of each glass and dip in salt. Place one lime half-round on each glass for decoration.

Serve chilled.

Pineapple-Mango Rum

MAKES 20 GLASSES

Preparation: 10 minutes

EQUIPMENT

Muddler

Cocktail spoon

Knife

INGREDIENTS

6¾ fl oz (20 cl) white rum

20 mint leaves

Around 20 ice cubes

34 fl oz (1 l) mango juice, chilled

34 fl oz (1 l) pineapple juice, chilled

2 cold limes

1 cold pineapple

1 cold mango

Pour the rum into a large bowl.

Wash and dry the mint leaves. Add to the bowl with the rum and crush with a muddler to extract as much flavor as possible. Add the ice cubes to the bowl. Add the juices. Stir with a cocktail spoon.

Wash and slice the limes. Peel the pineapple and cut into pieces. Wash the mango and cut into thin slices to decorate the bowl. Add the pineapple pieces and lime slices to the cocktail and stir again.

Serve chilled.

Alcohol-Free Version

INGREDIENTS

20 mint leaves

Around 20 ice cubes

6¾ fl oz (20 cl) tonic water, chilled

34 fl oz (1 l) mango juice, chilled

34 fl oz (1 l) pineapple juice, chilled

2 cold limes

1 cold pineapple

1 cold mango

Wash and dry the mint leaves. Add to the bowl and crush with a muddler to extract as much flavor as possible. Add the ice cubes to the bowl. Pour in the tonic and juices. Stir with a cocktail spoon.

Wash and slice the limes. Peel the pineapple and cut into pieces. Wash the mango and cut into thin slices to decorate the bowl. Add the pineapple pieces and lime slices to the cocktail and stir again.

Serve chilled.

Blue Lemonade

MAKES 10 GLASSES

Preparation: 5 minutes

EQUIPMENT

Cocktail spoon

Blender

Knife

INGREDIENTS

Around 20 ice cubes

10 fl oz (30 cl) gin

10 fl oz (30 cl) blue curaçao

5 fl oz (15 cl) lemon juice, chilled

25 fl oz (75 cl) lemonade, chilled

5 cold lemons

Blend the ice cubes to make crushed ice.

Put the crushed ice in a large bowl. Pour in the gin and curaçao. Add the lemon juice and the lemonade. Stir with a cocktail spoon.

Rinse and slice the lemons and add to the bowl.

Serve chilled.

Alcohol-Free Version

INGREDIENTS

Around 20 ice cubes

10 fl oz (30 cl) blue curaçao syrup (or mint)

5 fl oz (15 cl) lemon juice, chilled

34 fl oz (1 l) lemonade, chilled

5 cold lemons

Blend the ice cubes to make crushed ice.

Put the crushed ice in a large bowl. Pour in the syrup and lemon juice. Add the lemonade. Stir with a cocktail spoon.

Rinse and slice the lemons and add to the bowl.

Serve chilled.

Pomegranate Paloma

MAKES 10 GLASSES

Preparation: 10 minutes

EQUIPMENT

Blender

Cocktail spoon

Grater

Citrus reamer

Knife

INGREDIENTS

Around 20 ice cubes

13½ fl oz (40 cl) tequila

6¾ fl oz (20 cl) pink grapefruit juice, chilled

6¾ fl oz (20 cl) pomegranate juice, chilled

6¾ fl oz (20 cl) sparkling water, chilled

2 cold limes

1 cold grapefruit

1 cold pomegranate

Blend the ice cubes to make crushed ice. Place into a large bowl.

Pour the tequila, grapefruit juice, and pomegranate juice into the bowl. Stir with a cocktail spoon. Finish the cocktail with sparkling water.

Wash the limes and grate wide strips of peel before juicing them. Add the peel and juice to the cocktail. Wash the grapefruit and cut into rounds. Cut the pomegranate in half and remove the seeds. Add the grapefruit rounds and pomegranate seeds to the cocktail.

Serve chilled.

Alcohol-Free Version

INGREDIENTS

Around 20 ice cubes

6¾ fl oz (20 cl) tonic water, chilled

10 fl oz (30 cl) pink grapefruit juice, chilled

10 fl oz (30 cl) pomegranate juice, chilled

6¾ fl oz (20 cl) sparkling water, chilled

2 cold limes

1 cold grapefruit

1 cold pomegranate

Blend the ice cubes to make crushed ice. Place into a large bowl.

Pour the tonic, grapefruit juice, and pomegranate juice into the bowl. Stir with a cocktail spoon. Finish the cocktail with sparkling water.

Wash the limes and grate wide strips of peel before juicing them. Add the peel and juice to the cocktail. Wash the grapefruit and cut into rounds. Cut the pomegranate in half and remove the seeds. Add the grapefruit rounds and pomegranate seeds to the cocktail.

Serve chilled.

Cucumber-Watermelon Martini

MAKES 10 GLASSES

Preparation: 10 minutes

EQUIPMENT

Blender

Cocktail spoon

Knife

INGREDIENTS

3 cold cucumbers

1 cold watermelon

Around 20 ice cubes

17 fl oz (50 cl) vodka

10 fl oz (30 cl) Martini® rosé

Peel 2 of the cucumbers. Cut the watermelon and blend the flesh after removing the seeds. Add the cucumbers to the blender and blend again.

Place the ice cubes in a large bowl. Pour in the vodka and Martini® rosé. Add the cucumber-watermelon juice. Stir with a cocktail spoon.

Wash the remaining cucumber and slice in rounds. Add to the bowl.

Serve chilled.

Alcohol-Free Version

INGREDIENTS

3 cold cucumbers

1 cold watermelon

Around 20 ice cubes

10 fl oz (30 cl) red grape juice, chilled

3⅓ fl oz (10 cl) cucumber or watermelon syrup

13½ fl oz (40 cl) sparkling water, chilled

Peel 2 of the cucumbers. Cut the watermelon and blend the flesh after removing the seeds. Add the cucumbers to the blender and blend again.

Place the ice cubes in a large bowl. Pour in the grape juice, syrup, and cucumber-watermelon juice. Finish with the sparkling water. Stir with a cocktail spoon.

Wash the remaining cucumber and slice in rounds. Add to the bowl.

Serve chilled.

Piña Colada

MAKES 10 GLASSES

Preparation: 10 minutes

EQUIPMENT

Whisk

Knife

INGREDIENTS

13½ fl oz (40 cl) white rum

8½ fl oz (25 cl) dark rum

40½ fl oz (1.2 l) pineapple juice, chilled

13½ fl oz (40 cl) coconut milk, chilled

Around 20 ice cubes

1 cold pineapple

Pour the rums, pineapple juice, and coconut milk into a large bowl. Mix with a whisk until combined. Add the ice cubes. Whisk vigorously until you have a foamy texture.

Peel and cut the pineapple. Add pineapple pieces to the cocktail.

Serve chilled.

Alcohol-Free Version

INGREDIENTS

6¾ fl oz (20 cl) rum-flavored syrup or red sugarcane syrup

51 fl oz (1.5 l) pineapple juice, chilled

17 fl oz (50 cl) coconut milk, chilled

Around 20 ice cubes

1 cold pineapple

Pour the syrup, pineapple juice, and coconut milk into a large bowl. Mix with a whisk until combined. Add the ice cubes. Whisk vigorously until you have a foamy texture.

Peel and cut the pineapple. Add pineapple pieces to the cocktail.

Serve chilled.

...SWEET DELIGHTS

Watermelon and Honey Sangria

SERVES 10

Preparation: 5 minutes

Freezing: 2 hours

EQUIPMENT

Melon baller

Cocktail spoon

Citrus reamer

Knife

INGREDIENTS

¼ watermelon

1 honeydew melon

1 cantaloupe melon

4 cold limes

34 fl oz (1 l) white wine, chilled

5 fl oz (15 cl) gin

2 tbsp honey

17 fl oz (50 cl) lemonade, chilled

Use the melon baller to scoop out balls of watermelon, honeydew, and cantaloupe. Place these in the freezer for at least 2 hours to make ice cubes.

Juice 2 limes and slice the other 2 into thin rounds. Pour the white wine, gin, and lime juice into a large bowl. Mix, then add the honey. Mix again.

Add the fruit ice cubes and lime rounds to the bowl. Finish with the lemonade.

Serve chilled.

Alcohol-Free Version

INGREDIENTS

¼ watermelon

1 honeydew melon

1 cantaloupe melon

4 cold limes

34 fl oz (1 l) white grape juice, chilled

5 fl oz (15 cl) tonic water, chilled

2 tbsp honey

17 fl oz (50 cl) lemonade, chilled

Use the melon baller to scoop out balls of watermelon, honeydew, and cantaloupe. Place these in the freezer for at least 2 hours to make ice cubes.

Juice 2 limes and slice the other 2 into thin rounds. Pour the white grape juice, tonic, and lime juice into a large bowl. Mix, then add the honey. Mix again.

Add the fruit ice cubes and lime rounds to the bowl. Finish with the lemonade.

Serve chilled.

Minty-Melon Limoncello

MAKES 10 GLASSES

Preparation: 10 minutes

EQUIPMENT

Muddler

Cocktail spoon

Knife

Melon baller

INGREDIENTS

17 fl oz (50 cl) limoncello

20 mint leaves

Around 20 ice cubes

25 fl oz (75 cl) pinot grigio
(white wine), chilled

2 cold melons

1 cold cucumber

Pour the limoncello into a large bowl.

Wash and dry the mint leaves. Add them to the bowl and muddle to extract as much flavor as possible. Add the ice cubes and the pinot grigio. Stir with a cocktail spoon.

Cut the melons in half, remove the seeds, and use the melon baller to scoop out the flesh. Wash the cucumber and slice into rounds. Add the cucumber rounds and melon balls to the cocktail.

Serve chilled.

Alcohol-Free Version

INGREDIENTS

13½ fl oz (40 cl) lemon juice,
chilled

3⅓ fl oz (10 cl) sugarcane syrup

20 mint leaves

Around 20 ice cubes

25 fl oz (75 cl) white grape juice,
chilled

2 cold melons

1 cold cucumber

Pour the lemon juice and sugarcane syrup into a large bowl.

Wash and dry the mint leaves. Add them to the bowl and muddle to extract as much flavor as possible. Add the ice cubes and white grape juice. Stir with a cocktail spoon.

Cut the melons in half, remove the seeds, and use the melon baller to scoop out the flesh. Wash the cucumber and slice into rounds. Add the cucumber rounds and melon balls to the cocktail.

Serve chilled.

Pink Elephant

MAKES 10 GLASSES

Preparation: 5 minutes

EQUIPMENT

Cocktail spoon

Knife

INGREDIENTS

Around 20 ice cubes

6¾ fl oz (20 cl) Grand Marnier®

6¾ fl oz (20 cl) white rum

3⅓ fl oz (10 cl) strawberry syrup

34 fl oz (1 l) grapefruit juice, chilled

2 cold limes

Strawberry-flavored pink gummy candies

Place the ice cubes in a large bowl. Pour in the Grand Marnier® and white rum. Add the strawberry syrup and grapefruit juice. Stir with a cocktail spoon.

Wash the limes and slice into rounds. Add to the cocktail. Stir.

Serve chilled with a few pink candies.

Alcohol-Free Version

INGREDIENTS

Around 20 ice cubes

10 fl oz (30 cl) tonic water, chilled

3⅓ fl oz (10 cl) orange syrup

3⅓ fl oz (10 cl) strawberry syrup

34 fl oz (1 l) grapefruit juice, chilled

2 cold limes

Strawberry-flavored pink gummy candies

Place the ice cubes in a large bowl. Pour in the tonic and syrups. Add the grapefruit juice. Stir with a cocktail spoon.

Wash the limes and slice into rounds. Add to the cocktail. Stir.

Serve chilled with a few pink candies.

Raspberry Limoncello Sorbet

MAKES 10 GLASSES

Preparation: 5 minutes

EQUIPMENT

Cocktail spoon

Knife

Ice cream scoop

INGREDIENTS

Around 20 ice cubes

34 fl oz (1 l) prosecco, chilled

17 fl oz (50 cl) limoncello

2 cold lemons

1 cold pineapple

1 container raspberry sorbet

Place the ice cubes in a large bowl. Pour in the prosecco and limoncello. Stir with a cocktail spoon.

Wash the lemons and slice into thin rounds. Peel the pineapple and cut into pieces. Add all of the fruit to the cocktail.

Serve chilled, adding 1 scoop of raspberry sorbet to each glass when serving.

Alcohol-Free Version

INGREDIENTS

Around 20 ice cubes

34 fl oz (1 l) lemonade, chilled

10 fl oz (30 cl) lemon juice, chilled

6¾ fl oz (20 cl) sugarcane syrup

2 cold lemons

1 cold pineapple

1 container raspberry sorbet

Place the ice cubes in a large bowl. Pour in the lemonade, lemon juice, and sugarcane syrup. Stir with a cocktail spoon.

Wash the lemons and slice into thin rounds. Peel the pineapple and cut into pieces. Add all of the fruit to the cocktail.

Serve chilled, adding 1 scoop of raspberry sorbet to each glass when serving.

Caramel Milkshake

MAKES 10 GLASSES

Preparation: 10 minutes

EQUIPMENT

Whisk

INGREDIENTS

8½ fl oz (25 cl) caramel liqueur

8½ fl oz (25 cl) Amaretto

13½ fl oz (40 cl) milk, chilled

13½ fl oz (40 cl) heavy cream, chilled

Around 20 ice cubes

Fleur de sel (substitute sea salt, if not available)

5 rosemary sprigs

1 bottle salted caramel sauce

Pour the caramel liqueur, Amaretto, milk, and heavy cream into a large bowl. Whisk until combined. Add the ice cubes. Whisk vigorously until you have a foamy texture. Finish with a few pinches of *fleur de sel* and rosemary sprigs.

When serving, line the inside of each glass with caramel sauce before adding the cocktail for even more of a treat.

Alcohol-Free Version

INGREDIENTS

5 fl oz (15 cl) caramel syrup

5 fl oz (15 cl) orgeat syrup

17 fl oz (50 cl) milk, chilled

17 fl oz (50 cl) heavy cream, chilled

Around 20 ice cubes

Fleur de sel (substitute sea salt, if not available)

5 rosemary sprigs

1 bottle salted caramel sauce

Pour the syrups, milk, and heavy cream into a large bowl. Whisk until combined. Add the ice cubes. Whisk vigorously until you have a foamy texture. Finish with a few pinches of *fleur de sel* and rosemary sprigs.

When serving, line the inside of each glass with caramel sauce before adding the cocktail for even more of a treat.

Lava Flow

MAKES 10 GLASSES

Preparation: 10 minutes

EQUIPMENT

Blender

Knife

INGREDIENTS

18 oz (500 g) cold strawberries

Around 20 ice cubes

20 fl oz (60 cl) white rum

20 fl oz (60 cl) pineapple juice, chilled

20 fl oz (60 cl) coconut cream

5 cold bananas

1 Queen Victoria pineapple

Remove the strawberry stems and blend the fruit with the rum and a few ice cubes.

Place the rest of the ice cubes in a large bowl. Pour in the strawberry-rum mixture.

Rinse the blender and blend the pineapple juice with the coconut cream and bananas. Slowly pour the mixture into the bowl to create a "lava flow" effect.

Remove the pineapple ends and slice without peeling. Use small pineapple slices to decorate each glass.

Serve chilled.

Alcohol-Free Version

INGREDIENTS

18 oz (500 g) cold strawberries

3⅓ fl oz (10 cl) strawberry syrup

Around 20 ice cubes

30 fl oz (90 cl) pineapple juice, chilled

27 fl oz (80 cl) coconut cream, chilled

5 cold bananas

1 Queen Victoria pineapple

Remove the strawberry stems and blend the fruit with the strawberry syrup and a few ice cubes.

Place the rest of the ice cubes in a large bowl. Pour in the strawberry mixture.

Rinse the blender and blend the pineapple juice with the coconut cream and bananas. Slowly pour the mixture into the bowl to create a "lava flow" effect.

Remove the pineapple ends and slice without peeling. Use small pineapple slices to decorate each glass.

Serve chilled.

Little Tips and Extras

If you don't drink alcohol, replace . . .

Rum	with ginger syrup
Gin	with Canada Dry®
Tequila	with peppermint essential oil
Whiskey	with coffee syrup
You can also use spice or herb syrups (cinnamon, tarragon, anise, chili pepper . . .)	
Or alcohol-flavored syrups (mojito, gin, piña colada, curaçao . . .)	

To personalize your cocktail:

Flower waters	Orange flower water, rose water
Essential oils	Lavender, fennel, rosemary, sage, geranium, peppermint
Aromatic herbs	Basil, rosemary, tarragon, mint, thyme, dill
Bitters	Suze®, Jägermeister®, Picon®, Angostura
"Vintage" alcohols	Chartreuse, absinthe
Fruits and vegetables	Rhubarb, kiwi, cucumber, grated ginger
Candied fruits	Cherries in *eau-de-vie*, apricots, clementines, orange and lemon peels
Olives	Pimento-stuffed olives
Shaken egg white	
Syrups with unique flavors	Violet, rose, poppy, lavender
Zests	Lemon, lime, orange, kumquat
Sweeteners	Honey, maple syrup

Index

Émilie Laraison would like to thank Natacha, Marie, and Zélie for their help.

Skyhorse Publishing books may be purchased in bulk at special discounts for sales promotion, corporate gifts, fund-raising, or educational purposes. Special editions can also be created to specifications. For details, contact the Special Sales Department, Skyhorse Publishing, 307 West 36th Street, 11th Floor, New York, NY 10018 or info@skyhorsepublishing.com.

Visit our website at www.skyhorsepublishing.com.

10 9 8 7 6 5 4 3 2 1

Library of Congress Cataloging-in-Publication Data is available on file.

Editorial director: Didier Férat
Editing: Diane Monserat
Graphics: Julia Philipps
Photography by Émilie Laraison

Layout and photoengraving: Nord Compo
Manufacturing: Laurence Duboscq
Translation by Grace McQuillan

ISBN: 978-1-5107-6128-5
eISBN: 978-1-5107-6182-7

Printed in China